Tennessee

Jim Ollhoff

Visit us at
www.abdopublishing.com

Published by ABDO Publishing Company, 8000 West 78th Street, Suite 310, Edina, Minnesota 55439 USA. Copyright ©2010 by Abdo Consulting Group, Inc. International copyrights reserved in all countries. No part of this book may be reproduced in any form without written permission from the publisher. The Checkerboard Library™ is a trademark and logo of ABDO Publishing Company.

Printed in the United States.

Editor: John Hamilton
Graphic Design: Sue Hamilton
Cover Illustration: Neil Klinepier
Cover Photo: iStock Photo

Manufactured with paper containing at least 10% post-consumer waste

Interior Photo Credits: AirPhoto-Jim Wark, Alamy, AP Images, Brian Stansberry, Corbis, Getty, Granger Collection, iStock Photo, John Hamilton, Jupiterimages, Library of Congress, McClung Museum-Univ of Tennessee-Greg Harlin, Memphis Grizzlies, Mile High Maps, Mountain High Maps, Nashville Predators, One Mile Up, Peter Arnold Inc., Tennessee Titans, and the Water Valley Casey Jones Railroad Museum Web Site.
Statistics: State population statistics taken from 2008 U.S. Census Bureau estimates. City and town population statistics taken from July 1, 2007, U.S. Census Bureau estimates. Land and water area statistics taken from 2000 Census, U.S. Census Bureau.

Library of Congress Cataloging-in-Publication Data

Ollhoff, Jim, 1959-
  Tennessee / Jim Ollhoff.
      p. cm. -- (The United States)
  Includes index.
  ISBN 978-1-60453-678-2
  1. Tennessee--Juvenile literature. I. Title.

F436.3.O45 2009
976.8--dc22
                              2008052876

Table of Contents

The Volunteer State

Tennessee lies between the Mississippi River and the Appalachian Mountains. Its early pioneers developed a frontier spirit that still survives today. Many Tennesseans live on farms and rural areas. However, since the 1940s the state has attracted many manufacturing businesses.

Tennessee is famous for its music, especially country, blues, and jazz. Elvis Presley's home, Graceland, is in Memphis.

Tennessee's nickname is The Volunteer State. In the War of 1812, the governor of Tennessee asked volunteers to help defend the country from the British. Thousands of people volunteered for duty. In January 1815, Tennessee soldiers helped win an important battle, the Battle of New Orleans.

Veteran of the War of 1812, John Oliver built this cabin in the 1850s. Today, it is part of Great Smoky Mountains National Park.

Quick Facts

Name: *Tanasi* was the name of a Cherokee Native American village. The name was later used to describe the Tennessee River. Eventually, it represented the whole region.

State Capital: Nashville

Date of Statehood: June 1, 1796 (16th state)

Population: 6,214,888 (17th-most populous state)

Area (Total Land and Water): 42,143 sq miles (109,150 sq km), 36th-largest state

Largest City: Memphis, population 674,028

Nickname: The Volunteer State

Motto: Agriculture and Commerce

State Bird: Mockingbird

State Flower: Iris

Limestone

Agate

Tulip Poplar

Clingmans Dome

State Rocks: Limestone and Agate

State Tree: Tulip Poplar

State Songs: "My Homeland, Tennessee"; "When It's Iris Time in Tennessee"; "My Tennessee"; "Tennessee Waltz"; "Rocky Top"; "Tennessee"; "The Pride of Tennessee"; "A Tennessee Bicentennial Rap: 1796-1996"

Highest Point: Clingmans Dome, 6,643 ft (2,025 m)

Lowest Point: Mississippi River, 178 ft (54 m)

Average July Temperature: 75°F (24°C)

Record High Temperature: 113°F (45°C) in Perryville, August 9, 1930

Average January Temperature: 39°F (4°C)

Record Low Temperature: -32°F (-36°C) in Mountain City, December 30, 1917

Average Annual Precipitation: 53 inches (135 cm)

Number of U.S. Senators: 2

Number of U.S. Representatives: 9

U.S. Postal Service Abbreviation: TN

Geography

Tennessee is 432 miles (695 km) from west to east. It's only 112 miles (180 km) from north to south. On the west side of the state is the Mississippi River. On the east side is North Carolina. Kentucky and Virginia are to the north of the state. On the south side of Tennessee are the states of Mississippi, Alabama, and Georgia.

People often divide the state into three parts: Western, Eastern, and Middle Tennessee. Western Tennessee has slightly rolling hills. The land gets flat and swampy near the Mississippi River. A lot of cotton grows in Western Tennessee.

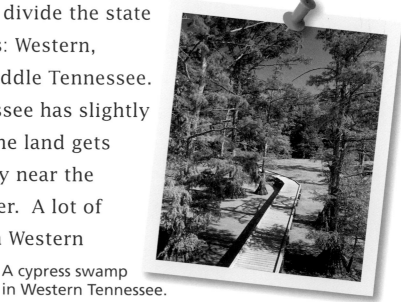

A cypress swamp in Western Tennessee.

Tennessee's total land and water area is 42,143 square miles (109,150 sq km). It is the 36th-largest state. The state capital is Nashville.

Sunrise over Great Smoky Mountain National Park in Eastern Tennessee.

Eastern Tennessee has the Great Smoky Mountains. These mountains are part of the Blue Ridge Mountain system, which is part of the Appalachian Mountains. There are 16 mountains that rise above 6,000 feet (1,829 m). The highest point in Tennessee, Clingmans Dome, is in this area.

Middle Tennessee has rolling hills and good soil for farming. Much of the agricultural land and many manufacturing businesses are in this area.

There are three major rivers in Tennessee. The Tennessee River begins near Knoxville, flows south into Alabama, and then loops back north toward Kentucky. The Mississippi River runs along the west side of the state. The Cumberland River loops into Tennessee through Nashville. Tennessee has dammed up many rivers, which has created 25 lakes. The largest natural lake in Tennessee is Reelfoot Lake. It is in the northwest corner of the state. It was created by the New Madrid Earthquakes of 1811 and 1812.

Reelfoot Lake is in the northwest corner of Tennessee.

Climate and Weather

A boy cools off in a fountain as hot, muggy summer weather hits Nashville.

Most of Tennessee has a humid, subtropical climate. It has hot summers and mild winters. Moist, southerly winds from the Gulf of Mexico affect Tennessee's climate. The state gets about 53 inches (135 cm) of precipitation yearly.

Average July temperatures in Tennessee range from 70 to 80 degrees Fahrenheit (21˚-27˚C). The temperature often gets higher than 95 degrees Fahrenheit (35˚C). Summer nights are warm and humid.

Winters are mild in Tennessee. Average temperatures range from 34 degrees Fahrenheit (1°C) in the east to 42 degrees Fahrenheit (6°C) in the west. In the central part of the state, daytime winter temperatures can rise to 50 degrees Fahrenheit (10°C). Winter temperatures of 0 degrees Fahrenheit (-18°C) usually only happen in the mountains.

Western Tennessee averages 5 inches (13 cm) of snow each year. Eastern Tennessee gets about 16 inches (41 cm) of snow.

A Knoxville snowstorm brings kids fun in Eastern Tennessee.

Plants and Animals

In the 1700s, forests covered almost all of Tennessee. Today, about half of the state is forested. There are almost 200 species of trees in the state. These trees include spruce, locust, poplar, ash, beech, maple, pine, oak, elm, walnut, and hickory. In the swampy areas of Western Tennessee, common trees are bald cypress, black willows, sweet gums, and river birches. The tulip poplar is the state tree. It was chosen as the state tree because it grows all over Tennessee, and because the pioneers used it for many of their building projects.

Tulip tree

Hikers pause to look at some towering trees on the Chimney Tops Trail in Great Smoky Mountains National Park. Trees once nearly filled the state of Tennessee. Today, about half the state remains forested.

Large animals in Tennessee include the white-tailed deer, cougar, and black bear. Smaller animals include beaver, mink, opossum, skunk, fox, and muskrat. The southern flying squirrel is found in the state. The flying squirrel doesn't really fly, but glides as it falls. The raccoon is Tennessee's official wild animal.

Many amphibians and reptiles are found in the state. Poisonous snakes include the copperhead, rattlesnake, and cottonmouth. Other snakes include the garter snake, king snake, black racer, and water snake. Salamanders, frogs, toads, and turtles are some of the other amphibians and reptiles. The official state reptile is the eastern box turtle.

Tennessee birds include bluebird, duck, grouse, hawk, robin, wild turkey, and many others. The mockingbird is the official state bird.

Black bears still roam the wilderness of Tennessee.

Deer

Flying Squirrel

Eastern Box Turtle

History

People have lived in the Tennessee area for at least 12,000 years. Before the arrival of Europeans, there were several Native American tribes. The Shawnee left the area when the first European settlers arrived. The Chickasaw claimed the west side of Tennessee. The Yuchi and Creek tribes lived in the southeast part of the state. The Cherokee lived in the large middle section of the state.

Spanish explorer Hernando de Soto was probably the first European to visit Tennessee. He explored the area in 1540.

Hernando de Soto
sees the Mississippi River in 1541.

On February 10, 1763, representatives of France, Great Britain, Spain, and Portugal signed the Treaty of Paris. This ended the French and Indian War, and gave control of many areas of America to King George III of Great Britain.

In the 1600s, both Great Britain and France claimed land that included Tennessee, even though Native Americans were still living there. In 1763, Great Britain gained control of the land in an agreement called the Treaty of Paris. The area of Tennessee became part of the English colony of North Carolina.

Starting in the late 1760s and 1770s, settlers built forts that eventually became towns. The area became an official territory of the United States in 1790. Tennessee joined the Union as the 16th state in 1796.

By 1840, most Native Americans had been forced out of Tennessee. This brought more settlers. Railroads were built that brought people and products in and out of Tennessee.

A Cumberland Valley settlement is attacked. By 1840, most Native Americans had been forced out of Tennessee.

Slavery divided the United States in the mid-1800s. Southern states had large plantations. Slaves were used to work the fields. Many people, especially in Northern states, wanted to end slavery.

The Battle of Chattanooga in November 1863 was a turning point in the war. Union troops defeated the Confederate forces, opening a way into Georgia.

In 1861, 11 Southern states, including Tennessee, withdrew from the United States. They formed the Confederacy. The Civil War between North and South began. More than 200 battles were fought in Tennessee.

The Civil War caused much destruction. After the war ended in 1865, it was a time known as Reconstruction. This was a hard time for people in Tennessee. Many were homeless and without jobs.

During World War I (1914-1918), the United States military had many needs. This brought jobs to Tennessee. Many companies helped with the war effort.

In 1929, the Great Depression began. This was a time when people had trouble finding jobs, and many people were without money or work. The

Great Depression hit Tennessee very hard. However, in 1933, the United States government started a plan in Tennessee. It was called the Tennessee

Valley Authority. It worked to develop natural resources, such as building dams on rivers. This brought many jobs to Tennessee, and helped the

state's economy for decades.

Many people were employed by the Tennessee Valley Authority to build the Watts Bar Dam and other projects around the state.

Oak Ridge National Laboratories in 1945.

When America fought in World War II (1939-1945), the United States government built the Oak Ridge National Laboratories. It helped build the atomic bombs that brought an end to the war.

Since the 1960s, many businesses have moved to Tennessee. There is now a wide variety of businesses and corporations in the state.

Did You Know?

The Cherokee were one of the largest Native American tribes. Many Cherokee lived in the area that would later become the state of Tennessee. Cherokee were usually peaceful to American settlers. They began to adopt some of the ways of the settlers in order to live in peace. Many Cherokee became farmers. A Cherokee man named Sequoyah created an alphabet in their native

Sequoyah

language. Other Cherokee took jobs. Cherokee leaders signed treaties with the white settlers. However, settlers continued to stream into Tennessee. They wanted the land of the Cherokee. Many of the Cherokee resisted.

In 1838, the U.S. military began forcing Cherokee families from their ancestral homes. They were held in camps for weeks, often with no food or shelter. Then, the military made them move to Oklahoma. Of the 15,000 men, women, and children who were forced to walk to Oklahoma, more than 4,000 died along the way. This march today is called the Trail of Tears.

Trail of Tears

People

Casey Jones (1863?-1900) was a railroad engineer who lived in Jackson, Tennessee. In April of 1900, he was driving his train through Mississippi. It was night, and very foggy, and he saw too late that there was a stopped train on the tracks. He blew the train whistle, which warned people. He slammed on the brakes. He told the others in the locomotive to jump off the train while he continued to try to stop it. His train crashed into the other train, but Jones had slowed the train down a lot. Casey Jones was the only one who died in the crash. His heroism was made popular by a song, "The Ballad of Casey Jones."

Al Gore (1948-) was born in Washington, D.C., while his father was a senator from Tennessee. Al Gore served in the House of Representatives, and also became a senator for Tennessee. He was the vice-president of the United States from 1993-2001. He ran for president in 2000. He has always been interested in

environmental issues. His crusade for awareness of global climate change earned him the Nobel Peace Prize in 2007.

Aretha Franklin
(1942-) was born in Memphis, Tennessee. She is known as "The Queen of Soul" because she is famous for singing soul music. She began to sing in the early 1960s. In 1987, she became the first woman to be inducted into the Rock and Roll Hall of Fame. She has won 20 Grammy Awards. One of her most famous songs is "Respect." In 2009, she was the featured singer at the presidential inauguration of Barack Obama.

Davy Crockett (1786-1836) was born on the very eastern edge of Tennessee, probably near today's town of Limestone Cove. He was a frontiersman, trapper, politician, and soldier. Sometimes he is called "King of the Wild Frontier." He represented Tennessee in the United States House of Representatives. He died in Texas at the Battle of the Alamo.

Cities

Nashville is the capital of Tennessee. It was settled by Europeans in the 1770s. It is the state's second-

biggest city. However, when all the area suburbs and towns are counted, the Nashville area has more than 1.5 million people. That makes it the biggest metropolitan area in the state. Nashville has many manufacturing and trade businesses. It is also an important music-recording center. Tennessee State University is in Nashville.

Memphis is the largest city in Tennessee, with a population of 674,028. It is a major port for

traffic on the Mississippi River. The National Civil Rights Museum is in Memphis. This marks the site where Martin Luther King was killed in 1968. Memphis was first visited by Europeans in 1541, when Hernando de Soto explored the area. Andrew Jackson, who became the seventh president of the United States, helped to start the town in 1819. The University of Memphis is one of several colleges in the city.

Knoxville is located in the east side of the state, along the Tennessee River. Its population is 183,546. The first non-Indian settlement in the area was a fort built in 1786. Today, tourism is important in the city. Great Smoky Mountains National Park is nearby, along with other historic sites and recreation areas. The University of Tennessee, which began in 1794, is in Knoxville.

Chattanooga is the fourth-largest city in Tennessee, with a population of 169,884. It lies in the southeast corner of the state. The city's name was probably taken from the language of a Native American tribe. The site was settled by pioneers in the early 1800s. Today, the city enjoys a mix of service and manufacturing industries. It is also home to the Hunter Museum of American Art, the Tennessee Aquarium, the Chattanooga Theatre Center, and the Chattanooga Symphony and Opera.

Transportation

Interstate 40 is the main east-west road across Tennessee. Interstates 24 and 65 cross north and south through Nashville. Interstate 75 goes

north and south through Knoxville. Tennessee has more than 85,000 miles (136,794 km) of roads.

The state has about 2,600 miles (4,184 km) of railroad tracks. Railroads are important for hauling freight. The main railroad centers are in Memphis and Nashville.

A barge transports goods on the Mississippi River, while a truck travels over the I-155 bridge in Dyer County, Tennessee. Many products make their way across the state.

The city of Memphis sits along the Mississippi River, and is the state's biggest port. Many products are loaded and unloaded in Memphis. Nashville has a port along the Cumberland River. Chattanooga is an important port on the Tennessee River.

Tennessee has more than 200 airports and heliports. The biggest airports are in Nashville and Memphis.

Natural Resources

There are about 79,000 farms in Tennessee. Soybeans are the main farm crop. Soybeans are used for livestock feed, paints, ink, and even medicines.

Cotton is another important crop in Tennessee. Most cotton is used for cloth and clothing, but some of it is used for plastics and for livestock feed. Other farm crops include vegetables, tobacco, and strawberries.

Soybeans, cotton, tobacco, and strawberries are grown in Tennessee.

Tennessee farmers raise more than two million chickens each year. Those chickens produce

Tennessee farmers raise more than two million chickens each year.

more than 278 million eggs. Farmers raise more than two million cattle in Tennessee each year. There are many dairy farmers in the state.

Tennessee has many minerals. Coal is plentiful in the eastern part of the state. Copper, zinc, and precious gems can also be found in Tennessee.

Industry

Tennessee was mostly an agricultural state until the mid-1900s. In the 1930s, during the Great Depression, the United States government formed a corporation called the Tennessee Valley Authority. It provided electricity, and also helped with flood control and general economic development. With the electricity from the Tennessee Valley Authority, the state was able to attract more manufacturing companies.

Manufacturing continues to be the main part of Tennessee's economy. Chemicals, clothing, and industrial machinery are important manufactured products. Other goods include food, rubber products, aluminum, and print products.

Tennessee's Dollywood amusement park welcomes about 6 million people each season.

Tourism is increasingly important. About 40 million travelers each year visit Tennessee. Great Smoky Mountains National Park, historic sites, and state parks are popular attractions. The music industry also attracts many tourists.

Sports

The Tennessee Titans are the state's National Football League team. The Titans moved to the state in 1997. They play at LP Field in Nashville. The Nashville Predators are the state's National Hockey League team. The Memphis Grizzlies play professional basketball.

Tennessee is a stop on the NASCAR racing circuit. The state also has several minor league baseball teams. College and high school sports are very popular in Tennessee.

Tennessee has mountains and forests, which provide many opportunities for hiking, hunting, or wildlife watching. Great Smoky Mountains National Park and Cherokee National Forest are popular spots for outdoor lovers. Tennessee also has 53 state parks.

Hikers climb their way up Unaka Mountain in Cherokee National Forest near Unicoi, Tennessee.

Entertainment

There are many fairs and festivals happening year-round in Tennessee. The National Cornbread Festival is held every April in South Pittsburg. The West Tennessee Strawberry Festival is held in Humboldt. And residents of Paris, Tennessee, claim to have the world's biggest fish fry. Visitors eat more than six tons (5.4 metric tons) of catfish each year.

Nashville's Grand Ole Opry is a center for country music. Its weekly radio program has been broadcasting since 1925. There also many other concert halls and museums in Nashville.

Graceland was the home of Elvis Presley in the city of Memphis. Elvis was a famous singer who was often called The King of Rock and Roll. He died at Graceland in 1977, and was buried in a small cemetery on the grounds.

Graceland, the home and private cemetery of legendary musician Elvis Presley, brings thousands of visitors to the city of Memphis each year.

Timeline

Pre-1500s—Shawnee, Chickasaw, Creek, and Cherokee Native Americans settle in the Tennessee area.

1540—Spanish explorer Hernando de Soto explores the Tennessee area.

1763—England gains control of Tennessee.

1770s—Many settlers come to Tennessee.

1796—Tennessee becomes the 16th state in the Union.

1838—Native Americans are forced out of Tennessee in The Trail of Tears.

 **1861**—Tennessee withdraws from the Union. The Civil War begins.

 **1917-1918**—World War I brings many jobs to Tennessee.

 **1929**—The Great Depression begins. Tennessee's economy suffers greatly.

 **1941-1945**—America enters World War II. Oak Ridge National Laboratories is built in Tennessee.

 **1950s-1970s**—New businesses move to Tennessee, creating a stronger economy.

 **2008**—University of Tennessee Lady Vols win their 8th NCAA Women's Division I Basketball Championship.

Glossary

Appalachian Mountains—A mountain chain on the east side of Tennessee.

Civil War—The war fought between America's northern and southern states from 1861-1865. The southern states were for slavery. They wanted to start their own country. Northern states fought against slavery and a division of the country.

Elvis Presley—A famous American singer and actor known as the "King of Rock and Roll." He was born in Mississippi in 1935. He moved to Memphis, Tennessee, in 1948. He bought his mansion home, Graceland, and lived there until his death in 1977.

Graceland—The former mansion and current burial place of Elvis Presley in Memphis. Today, it is a popular tourist attraction, hosting about 600,000 visitors a year. It was declared a National Historic Landmark on March 27, 2006.

Great Depression—A time in American history beginning in 1929 and lasting for several years when many businesses failed and millions of people lost their jobs. The Great Depression hit Tennessee very hard.

New Madrid Earthquakes—A number of earthquakes that occurred in the New Madrid Seismic Zone in what is now the corners of Missouri, Arkansas, and Tennessee. It began with two very large quakes on December 16, 1811. Smaller aftershocks occurred in the weeks after. A final mega-quake shook the area on February 7, 1812.

Tennessee Valley Authority—A company established by Congress in May 1933 to develop the Tennessee River area. Many jobs were created. Dams and hydroelectric power plants were built, electrical lines were laid, and other development occurred because of the TVA.

Trail of Tears—The forced removal of the Cherokee and other Native American tribes to Oklahoma.

Index